First World War
and Army of Occupation
War Diary
France, Belgium and Germany

57 DIVISION
171 Infantry Brigade
King's (Liverpool Regiment)
2/7 Battalion
1 September 1915 - 29 February 1916

WO95/2982/1

The Naval & Military Press Ltd
www.nmarchive.com
Published in association with The National Archives

Published by

The Naval & Military Press Ltd

Unit 10 Ridgewood Industrial Park,

Uckfield, East Sussex,

TN22 5QE England

Tel: +44 (0) 1825 749494

www.naval-military-press.com

www.nmarchive.com

This diary has been reprinted in facsimile from the original. Any imperfections are inevitably reproduced and the quality may fall short of modern type and cartographic standards.

© **Crown Copyright**
Images reproduced by permission of The National Archives, London, England, 2015.

Contents

Document type	Place/Title	Date From	Date To
Heading	WO95/2982-1		
Heading	57th Division 171st Infy Bde 2-7th Bn King's Liverpool Regt 1915 Aug-1916 Feb And 1917 Feb 1919 May		
Heading	War Diary August 1915 2/7th Bn The King's (Liverpool Regiment)		
Miscellaneous	War Diary		
Heading	2/7th Bn The Kings (Liverpool Regiment) September 1915		
War Diary	Canterbury	01/09/1915	15/09/1915
War Diary	Petham	16/09/1915	16/09/1915
War Diary	Canterbury	23/09/1915	30/09/1915
Heading	2/7th The Kings (Liverpool Regiment) October 1915 Canterbury		
War Diary	Canterbury	06/10/1915	27/10/1915
Heading	2/7th Bn The Kings (Liverpool Regt) November 1915		
War Diary	Canterbury	01/11/1915	30/11/1915
Heading	2nd/7th Bn The Kings (Liverpool Regt) December 1915		
War Diary	Canterbury	01/12/1915	31/12/1915
Heading	2/7th Bn "The King's (Liverpool) Regt Canterbury January 1916		
War Diary	Canterbury	01/01/1916	31/01/1916
Heading	Diary 2/7th The Kings Liverpool Regt February 1916		
War Diary	Canterbury	01/02/1916	29/02/1916

m 05/10/28 (1)

mo 28/10 (1)

57TH DIVISION
171ST INFY BDE

2-7TH BN KING'S LIVERPOOL REGT
FEB 1917 - APR 1919

1915 AUG - 1916 FEB
AND
1917 FEB - 1919 MAY

Confidential War Diary.
                Summary.
        August. 1915.
2/7th Bn. The King's (Liverpool Regiment).

War Diary

Unit	2nd Line 7th Bn. King's L'pool Regt.
Brigade	171st Infantry Brigade
Division	57th (West Lancashire) Division
Mobilization Centre	Bootle, Liverpool. T.F.
Temporary War Station	Canterbury.

(a) Mobilization — No further experience.

(b) Concentration at War Station — No fresh circumstance to report.

(c) Organisation for defence. — No fresh circumstance to report.

(d) Training. — Company & Platoon Training has been carried out during the month, also musketry at SANDWICH.

(e) Discipline. — Is good.

(f) Administration.
1. Medical Services — Good
2. Veterinary " — Good
3. Supply " — Good
4. Transport " — Fair
5. Ordnance " — Good
6. Billeting & Hutting. Huts, Old Park Camp. Canterbury — Good
7. Channels of correspondence in routine matters. — Good
8. Range Construction — No experience
9. Supply of Remounts. — Nil.

(g) Reorganisation of T.F. into Home & Imperial Service. — No fresh circumstance to report.

(h) This Unit furnished 165 other ranks for overseas Force this month.

John W. Slater.
O/C. 2/7th Bn. THE KING'S (L'POOL REGT)

Army Form C. 2118.

WAR DIARY
or
INTELLIGENCE SUMMARY.
(Erase heading not required.)

2/7th Bn. The King's (Liverpool Regiment)

September 1915

Canterbury

Confidential

John A. Stables LT. COL.
o/c. 2/7th Bn. THE KING'S (L'POOL REGT.)

Army Form C. 2118.

2/7th Kings Liverpool Regt.

WAR DIARY
or
INTELLIGENCE SUMMARY.
(Erase heading not required.)

Instructions regarding War Diaries and Intelligence Summaries are contained in F.S. Regs., Part II and the Staff Manual respectively. Title pages will be prepared in manuscript.

Hour, Date, Place	Summary of Events and Information	Remarks and references to Appendices
8 PM Sept. 1 Canterbury	Night Operations	
7.15 AM " 2 Canterbury	Field Operations Outpost scheme	
9.30 AM " 8 Canterbury	Battalion moved into billets in CANTERBURY.	
2.30 PM " 15 Canterbury	Battalion bivouaced for the night at PETHAM.	
4.30 AM " 16 Petham	Field operations against 2/5th & 2/8th KLR.	
8.30 AM " 23 Canterbury	Field operations	
9.0 AM " 29 Canterbury	Field operations against Skeleton hostile forces at Petham. A Company took up outpost positions overnight	
9.15 AM " 30 Canterbury	Outpost scheme CHARTHAM DOWNS.	

John N. Stokes
LT. COL.
o/c. 2/7th Bn. THE KING'S (L'POOL REGT.)

Army Form C. 2118.

WAR DIARY
~~INTELLIGENCE SUMMARY~~
(Erase heading not required.)

Instructions regarding War Diaries and Intelligence Summaries are contained in F. S. Regs., Part II and the Staff Manual respectively. Title pages will be prepared in manuscript.

Hour, Date, Place	Summary of Events and Information	Remarks and references to Appendices

2nd/7th The Kings (Liverpool Regiment)

October 1915

Canterbury

Confidential

John M. Motlee Lt. Col.
O/C. 2/7th Bn. THE KING'S (L'POOL REGT.)

Army Form C. 2118.

WAR DIARY
or
INTELLIGENCE SUMMARY.
(Erase heading not required.)

2nd/7th Kings Liverpool Regt.

Hour, Date, Place	Summary of Events and Information	Remarks and references to Appendices
2.30 PM Oct 6 Canterbury	Special training to Officers & N.C.O's in Bomb throwing & trench fighting	
9.0 AM. Oct 8 Canterbury	Battalion moved into Hutments in Old Park.	
9.15 AM Oct 11 Canterbury	Field Operations at PATRIXBOURNE.	
8.0 PM Oct 12 Canterbury	Night Operations	
1.30 PM Oct 13 Canterbury	Battalion parade on Brigade Parade Ground, men qualified for Munition work parade on the night of line	
3.45 PM Oct 13 Canterbury	Fire Drill	
8.15 PM Oct 13 Canterbury	Zeppelins reported over FAVERSHAM.	
7.20 Oct 14 Canterbury	Fire Alarm: alight: outbreak of fire	
5.0 PM Oct 14 Canterbury	Lecture by Brigade Major to Officers & N.C.O's	
3.0 PM Oct 15 Canterbury	Garrison being Alarm	
9.15 AM Oct 20 Canterbury	Field Operations	
6.0 PM Oct 25 Canterbury	Night attack on Sussex Yeo. Trenches north of Camp	
Oct 27 Canterbury	2nd Lieut. C.P.L Knapp proceeded overseas	
10.30 PM Oct 29 Canterbury	Night Alarm	

John M. M^ccflen Lt. Col.
O/c, 2/7th Bn. THE KING'S (L'POOL REGT.)

Army Form C. 2118

WAR DIARY
or
INTELLIGENCE SUMMARY
(Erase heading not required.)

2/7th Bn: "The King's" (Liverpool Regt.)

November 1915.

Canterbury.

John M. Staten
Commanding

Confidential

A/8078
5/12/15

Army Form C. 2118

WAR DIARY
or
INTELLIGENCE SUMMARY
(Erase heading not required.)

Instructions regarding War Diaries and Intelligence Summaries are contained in F.S. Regs., Part II. and the Staff Manual respectively. Title Pages will be prepared in manuscript.

Place	Date	Hour	Summary of Events and Information	Remarks and references to Appendices
CANTERBURY	1915 Nov 1			
	2			
	3			
	4			
	5			
	6			
	7			
	8		10 Officers 4 N.C.O detailed for special intelligence duty at FORDWICH.	G.R.B Sheet 118 1"to 1 mile
	9		2 motor cars need from contractors	G.R.B.
	10		1st draft 12 ridinghorses transferred to 2/1 Bde R.F.A. ASH. 4 Heavy horses transferred to W.L.DIV. TRAIN	G.R.B.
	11			
	12			
	13			
	14			
	15		10 Remounts transferred to R.F.Corps	G.R.B
	16		3 " " " 209.959 rds · 256 Bde Reserve Amm" recd from 2/1 Bde RFA ASH.	G.R.B
	17		Inspection of Transport by Chief Inspector Q.M.G. Services. Report Satisfactory	G.R.B
	18		525 · 303 rifles received from WEEDON. in bad state of repair. Barrels worn, corroded + many minor defects.	
	19		517 " 256 " despatched to " " together with unserviceable bayonets and 105,625 rounds · 256 amm"	G.R.B
	20		209,959 rds · 256 amm" (Bde Reserve) despatched to C.O.O. WEEDON.	G.R.B
	21		15 Officers transferred to 3/4th The Kings BLACKPOOL. Battalion inspected by B'Gr. A.R.GILBERT D.S.O.	G.R.B
	22		Field telephone despatched to 3rd TUNBRIDGE WELLS SCHOOL OF INSTRUCTION	G.R.B
	23		6 G.S. wagons limbers F.N. sent to A.S.C for transfer in exchange for 6 G.S. wagons.	G.R.B
	24		Inspection of Battalion by Maj Gl. E.T.DICKSON INSPECTOR OF INFANTRY. Report unknown.	G.R.B
	25		2 officers 75 Other ranks attached to 1/1 Kent Cyclists for patrol duty MARGATE district.	G.R.B.
	26			
	27			
	28			
	29			
	30			

John N. Horton

WAR DIARY
or
INTELLIGENCE SUMMARY
(Erase heading not required.)

Army Form C. 2118

2nd/4th Bn. "The Kings" (Liverpool Regt.)

December 1915.

Canterbury.

Confidential.

Cosneyer hager for Lt. Col.
O/c, 2/7th Bn. THE KING'S (L'POOL REGT.)
Comm nding

Army Form C. 2118

WAR DIARY
or
~~INTELLIGENCE SUMMARY~~

(Erase heading not required.)

Instructions regarding War Diaries and Intelligence Summaries are contained in F. S. Regs., Part II. and the Staff Manual respectively. Title Pages will be prepared in manuscript.

Place	Date	Hour	Summary of Events and Information	Remarks and references to Appendices
	1915			
CANTERBURY	Dec 1			
	2			
	3			
	4			
	5			
	6		1 Officer & 22 other ranks proceeded to RYE for firing practice. (MACHINE GUN SECTION)	HD
	7			
	8			
	9			
	10		Draft of 84 Men left by 9.20 AM train for BLACKPOOL to 3/7th King's Liverpool	HD
	11			
	12			
	13			
	14			
	15			
	16			
	17			
	18			
	19			
	20			
	21			
	22		Inspection of all works &c including Quartermasters & Companies by Br.Gen. J R GILBERT D.S.O.	HD Satisfactory
	23		ARTILLERY formations under B.Gen J R GILBERT D.S.O.	HQ
	24		1 Light Draft-horse & 1 Pack pony. sent to 57th Wok Lancs Sick Lines with skin disease.	HD
	25			
	26			
	27			
	28		Inspection by Lieut General C L WOOLLCOMBE CB	HD Satisfactory
	29		1 Heavy Draft horse semi infoforced (sick)	HD
	30			
	31			

A S Meyer Major
for Lt. Col.
o/c 2/7th Bn THE KING'S (L'POOL R...)

Army Form C. 2118.

WAR DIARY
or
INTELLIGENCE SUMMARY.
(Erase heading not required.)

2/7th Bn "The King's (Liverpool) Regt.
Canterbury

January 1916

Confidential

Lt. Col: J.W. Slater V.D
Commanding

Place	Date	Hour	Summary of Events and Information	Remarks and references to Appendices

Army Form C. 2118

WAR DIARY
or
INTELLIGENCE SUMMARY
(Erase heading not required.)

17th Bn. The King's Liverpool Regiment.

Instructions regarding War Diaries and Intelligence Summaries are contained in F. S. Regs., Part II. and the Staff Manual respectively. Title Pages will be prepared in manuscript.

Place	Date	Hour	Summary of Events and Information	Remarks and references to Appendices
CANTERBURY	1.1.16		Headquarters nil	C.B.
	2		nil	C.B.
	3		nil	C.B.
	4		nil	C.B.
	5		nil	C.B.
	6		nil	C.B.
	7		nil	C.B.
	8		nil	C.B.
	9		nil C.B. 1 Officer 38 other ranks relieve 1 Officer 38 other ranks on detachment at RAMSGATE	C.B.
	10		nil	C.B.
	11		nil	C.B.
	12		nil	C.B.
	13		nil	C.B.
	14		2 Officers 74 other ranks rejoin from detachment duty at RAMSGATE	C.B.
	15		nil	C.B.
	16		nil	C.B.
	17		nil	C.B.
	18		nil	C.B.
	19		nil	C.B.
	20		nil	C.B.
	21		nil	C.B.
	22		68 recruits received from Administrative Centre Bootle	C.B.
	23		nil	C.B.
	24		nil	C.B.
	25		104 recruits received from Administrative Centre Bootle	C.B.
	26		nil	C.B.
	27		51 recruits received from Administrative Centre Bootle	C.B.
	28		nil	C.B.
	29		nil	C.B.
	30		nil	C.B.
	31		nil	C.B.

John M. Stables
Lt Col O/c 2/17th The King's L'pool Regt.

Army Form C. 2118

WAR DIARY
or
~~INTELLIGENCE SUMMARY~~
(Erase heading not required.)

Confidential Diary

2/7th The Kings Liverpool Regt.

February 1916.

Colonel J. W. Slater VD
Commanding.

Army Form C. 2118

WAR DIARY
or
INTELLIGENCE SUMMARY
(Erase heading not required.)

2/7th The Kings Khool Regt

Place	Date	Hour	Summary of Events and Information	Remarks and references to Appendices
CANTERBURY	1.2.16	nil		GioB
	2.2.16	nil		GioB
	3.	nil		GioB
	4	nil		GioB
	5	nil		GioB
	6	nil		5.B.
	7	nil		5.B.
	8	nil		6.B
	9	nil		6.B
	10	nil		6.B
	11	nil		6.B
	12	nil		6.B
	13	nil		6.B
	14	nil		9.B
	15	nil		6.B
	16	nil		5.B
	17	nil		5.B
	18	nil		6.B
	19	nil		6.B
	20	nil		5.B
	21	nil		5.B
	22	nil		6.B
	23	B'n res nil GeoB		
	24	11-18 AM	B'n rec'd orders to hold itself readiness tomorrow at short notice. 23 Officers 600 other ranks. 5.20 rifles strength.	6.B
	25		nil GeoB. B'n standby ready tomorrow 1 hours notice Machine gun handed over to 2/6 K.L.R.	6.B.
	26		Lewis machine gun rec'd from Granance. B'n standby ready to move 1 hour notice	6.B.
	27		nil GeoB B'n standby ready tomorrow 1 hour notice	5.B.
	28		— do —	5.B.
	29		— do —	6.B.

John D. Fowler
Lt Col Cdg 2/7 The Kings Khool Regt.

www.ingramcontent.com/pod-product-compliance
Lightning Source LLC
Chambersburg PA
CBHW081510160426
43193CB00014B/2643